A Note to Parents

DK READERS is a compelling program for beginning readers, designed in conjunction with leading literacy experts, including Dr. Linda Gambrell, Distinguished Professor of Education at Clemson University. Dr. Gambrell has served as President of the National Reading Conference, the College Reading Association, and the International Reading Association.

Beautiful illustrations and superb full-color photographs combine with engaging, easy-to-read stories to offer a fresh approach to each subject in the series. Each DK READER is guaranteed to capture a child's interest while developing his or her reading skills, general knowledge, and love of reading.

The five levels of DK READERS are aimed at different reading abilities, enabling you to choose the books that are exactly right for your child:

Pre-level 1: Learning to read
Level 1: Beginning to read
Level 2: Beginning to read alone
Level 3: Reading alone
Level 4: Proficient readers

The "normal" age at which a child begins to read can be anywhere from three to eight years old. Adult participation through the lower levels is very helpful for providing encouragement, discussing storylines, and sounding out unfamiliar words.

No matter which level you select, you can be sure that you are helping your child learn to read, then read to learn!

DK | Penguin Random House

Project Editor Susan Malyan
Art Editor C. David Gillingwater
Illustrator Peter Dennis
US Editor Adrienne Betz
Production Siu Chan
Jacket Designer Natalie Godwin
Editor, this edition Anneka Wahlhaus
Art Director Rachael Foster
Publishing Manager Bridget Giles

Dinosaur Consultant Angela Milner,
The Natural History Museum, London
Reading Consultant
Linda Gambrell, Ph.D.

First American edition, 2001
This edition, 2009
Published in the United States by DK Publishing
345 Hudson Street, New York, New York 10014

Copyright © 2001 Dorling Kindersley Limited
DK, a Division of Penguin Random House LLC
17 18 19 16 15 14
014–DD507–Sep/09

DK books are available at special discounts when purchased in bulk
for sales promotions, premiums, fund-raising, or educational use.
For details, contact: DK Publishing Special Markets
345 Hudson Street, New York, New York 10014
SpecialSales@dk.com

A catalog record for this book is available
from the Library of Congress

ISBN: 978-0-7566-5597-6 (pb)
ISBN: 978-0-7566-5598-3 (plc)

Printed and bound in U.S.A.

The publisher thanks the following for their kind permission
to reproduce their photographs:
c=center; t=top; b=bottom; l=left; r=right
CM Studios: 32-33c; **Corbis UK Ltd:** Bettmann/Corbis 20tl, 25tr,
26cl; Corbis 25cr; James L. Amos 41tr; Tom Bean/Corbis 28bl; **Mary
Evans Picture Library:** 4bl, 18tl, 20bc; **Robert Harding Picture
Library:** 7tr; **Royal Society:** 14t; **Kobal Collection:** 47tr;
Dreamworks/Paramount 45br; **The Natural History Museum,
London:** 4bc, 5br, 23b, 27tr, 40tl; **Topham Picturepoint:** 24bl.
Front jacket: Corbis: Louie Psihoyos crb.
DK Images: Senckenberg Nature Museum, Frankfurt t.
All other images © Dorling Kindersley Limited.

A WORLD OF IDEAS:
SEE ALL THERE IS TO KNOW

www.dk.com

Contents

DINOSAUR DETECTIVES

Written by Peter Chrisp

Dinosaur detectives

Long, long ago, people all over the world began finding huge bones buried in sand or stone. Sometimes, these findings gave rise to stories about giants and dragons.

Today, we know these bones belonged to enormous beasts who lived millions of years ago. Some of them were land reptiles, called dinosaurs. Dinosaurs walked the Earth for over 160 million years.

Mary Anning
One of the first fossil hunters, she discovered her first prehistoric creature when she was just 11 years old.
See page 6.

Gideon Mantell
This English doctor found a huge tooth. It led him on the trail of a beast he called Iguanodon.
See page 14.

Richard Owen
This brilliant scientist invented the word "dinosaur", and held a party inside a concrete model of one.
See page 20.

The dinosaurs died out 65 million years ago.

In this book, you can read about some of the people who first discovered the truth about these huge bones. Like detectives, they worked to collect evidence and put together clues.

What they learned gives us a picture of life in the far distant past, when our world was the home of the dinosaurs.

Othniel Marsh
This rich American and his rival Edward Cope hunted for fossils in the Wild West. They discovered and named many new kinds of dinosaur.
See page 28.

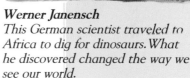

Werner Janensch
This German scientist traveled to Africa to dig for dinosaurs. What he discovered changed the way we see our world.
See page 34.

Jack Horner
This American scientist dug up dozens of dinosaur nests, many still containing eggs and babies.
See page 40.

The fossil woman

Welcome to my fossil shop! My name is Mary Anning. I've lived here in Lyme Regis all my life. I was born in 1799 above this very shop, where my father was a carpenter.

For six days of the week, Father worked hard, making furniture. But on Sundays, he would take me for walks along the beaches to look for fossils.

Fossils

Fossils are the remains of plants and animals, preserved in rock. Many fossils are bones which have gradually turned to stone.

He sold them to the ladies and gentlemen who come to the seaside every summer.

Father taught me how to tap a rock in just the right place with a hammer, to make it split open.

Often there would be nothing inside it. But sometimes we would find the skeleton of a beautiful fish, or a curly shell. We call the shells "snakestones" because they look like curled up snakes. Scientists call them ammonites.

The best time to find fossils is after a storm, when the wind and waves batter and chip away at the cliffs. When a storm hits Lyme Regis, all sorts of strange creatures just fall out of the cliffs.

Father said that we were "fishing for curiosities." It was a bit like fishing because we never knew what we would catch. But our "fish" were made of stone.

Lyme Regis
Lyme Regis, on the south coast of England, is still one of the best places in the world to find fossils.

Fossil seller
Mary Anning (1799–1847) was the first person to make a living by selling fossils.

Ammonites
These ancient relatives of the squid lived in the sea and caught food with their tentacles.

Fishing
Many people in Lyme Regis made their living from fishing in the sea.

Tools
Mary used simple tools, like this hammer and chisel, to split open rocks and chip out fossils.

My poor father died in 1810, when I was just ten years old. Mother made some money by selling fish, but it was not enough for us to live on.

I knew that I had to work to help feed my family. I decided that I would spend all my time looking for curiosities to sell.

One day, I was looking for fossils with my brother Joseph. Walking along the beach, I looked at the cliff and saw something wonderful staring back at me.

It was the skull of a strange animal. And what a skull!

It must have been about four feet (one meter) long, with a big round eye hole and jaws stuffed with sharp teeth.

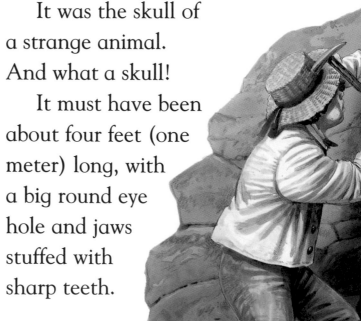

"It's a sea dragon, Mary!" said Joseph excitedly.

We hammered at the rocks until we could free the skull. Although it was very heavy, we managed to carry it home.

Joseph and I looked at pictures of animals in a book, to see if we could discover what it was. We decided that it must be a crocodile.

Seashells
Mary's fossil discoveries made her famous. The tongue twister, "She sells seashells on the sea shore" is thought to refer to her.

Geology
Geology, the study of the Earth and its rocks, was a new science in Mary's time.

Ichthyosaurus
This creature's name means "fish-reptile" in Greek.

I was sure that the rest of the crocodile was still there, buried in the cliff. All I had to do was wait for another rock slide. So after every storm, I would go back to the spot where we found the skull, hoping to see the rest of the skeleton.

It was almost a year later, in 1812, that the rocks finally fell away. There was my creature! But it wasn't a crocodile. Instead of legs, this animal had short paddles. It looked more like a fish!

I chipped the skeleton free with my hammer, and we carried it carefully back to our shop.

News quickly spread that the Annings had found a "sea dragon." Everyone wanted to have a look, and we were able to charge visitors some money to see it. Then we sold the skeleton to a local nobleman for £23 – more money than I'd ever seen before.

At this time, I met my first geologists – scientific gentlemen who came to see the creature and argue about what it was. One of these geologists, Mr. König, gave my creature a name: *Ichthyosaurus.*

Reptiles
Reptiles are the group of animals that includes lizards and snakes. *Ichthyosaurus* was a reptile that swam like a fish.

Naming
Scientists gave all plants and animals Greek or Latin names.

Artist's view
This etching from Mary's time shows the sea swarming with ichthyosaurs and plesiosaurs.

Sold for £100
In Mary's time, £100 was a huge sum of money. An ordinary family of five would be lucky to earn £1 in a week. Many people earned much less.

When I was 22, I found an even stranger creature in the cliffs. It had a tiny head, an amazingly long neck, and four flippers.

It took me months to chip it free from the rocks, but it was time well spent. I was able to sell it to the Duke of Buckingham for £100.

I showed the skeleton to a geologist called Mr. Conybeare, who visited me. His mouth dropped open in astonishment.

"I have never seen anything like this before!" he said. "It has the head of a turtle and the paddles of a whale. But its neck is like a giant snake. I shall call it *Plesiosaurus*, which means 'almost a reptile'."

Plesiosaurus made me famous, although some geologists accused me of having created a fake fossil to make money.

Then last year, I discovered a reptile with wings! A fossil expert called Professor Buckland has named it *Pterodactylus macronyx*. He says that the poor beast must have drowned in the sea.

Of course, finds such as these are very rare. Mostly, I live by selling ammonites. Would you like to buy one? ❖

Flying reptiles
Pterosaurs were flying reptiles which lived at the same time as the dinosaurs.

"Almost a reptile"
William Conybeare published a description of the *Plesiosaurus* in 1821. He apologized for giving it such a "vague name."

The strange tooth

Ladies and gentlemen, thank you for coming to my lecture! My name is Gideon Mantell. Today, I am going to tell you about a remarkable discovery that I made in 1822.

At the time, I was a doctor in the English county of Sussex. Although I practiced medicine, my real interest was in geology. Between visits to patients, I would always find time to collect fossils.

One spring day, I was visiting a patient with my wife, Mary Ann. She had come with me to enjoy the fine weather. While I was busy, she strolled down the lane and saw a pile of rocks, used by workmen to repair the roads.

In one of the rocks, my wife noticed something brown and shiny. Looking closely, she saw that it was a very large tooth.

And here is that tooth! As you can see, it is worn away on the side from chewing, like the tooth of a plant-eating mammal. But it is an odd shape, with ridges. I had never seen anything like it.

The workmen took me to the quarry, where I was amazed to learn that the tooth had come from a very old layer of rocks. No mammal fossil has ever been found in such rocks.

A fossilised Iguanodon *tooth*

Teeth
Tooth shapes show what an animal eats. Plant-eaters have short teeth for chopping and chewing leaves. Meat-eaters have sharp, jagged teeth.

Rock layers
Different types of fossils are found in different layers of rock. The oldest layers are the lowest in a rock face.

I knew of one man who might be able to help me solve the mystery of the tooth. Only Professor Buckland has a bigger collection of fossils than I do. He has spent years collecting them from quarries around England.

I traveled to the professor's home in Oxford, and showed him the enormous tooth.

"Remarkable, sir!" said Buckland. "I fear I cannot help you to identify it. But let me show you a fossil!"

He led me to his desk, piled high with a jumble of rocks. Buckland pulled out a large bone and handed it to me.

I could see that it was a jaw, for it held a long, sharp, curved tooth. "It looks like a flesh eater," I said, "a very big flesh eater!"

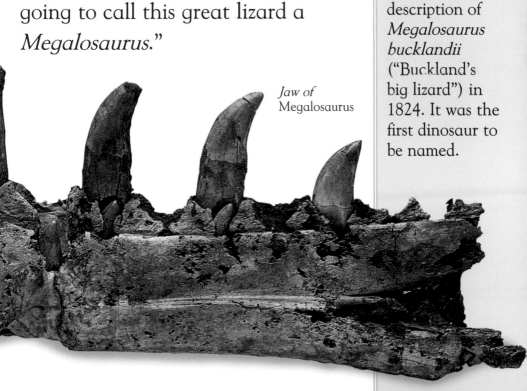

"It was found in a slate quarry not far from here," said Buckland. "As you will observe, it is shaped like a lizard's jaw. Yet from the size of the tooth, this lizard must have been more than 40 feet (12 meters) long.

Think of that, sir – a 40-foot (12-meter) long flesh-eating lizard roaming around Oxfordshire!" I shuddered at the thought of it.

The professor went on, "I am going to call this great lizard a *Megalosaurus*."

Jaw of Megalosaurus

Megalosaurus Buckland published a description of *Megalosaurus bucklandii* ("Buckland's big lizard") in 1824. It was the first dinosaur to be named.

Buckland invited me to stay for dinner, but I made excuses and left. I had heard that the professor ate odd things, like hedgehog meat.

As I traveled home, I thought about Buckland's discovery. I already knew of the giant sea reptiles discovered by Miss Anning at Lyme Regis. Now Buckland had found a huge land reptile.

Perhaps my tooth also came from an ancient reptile. Was it possible, I wondered, that before the time of the mammals, there had been an age of reptiles?

I found my next clue in 1825, at the museum of the Royal College of Surgeons in London.

Looking through the collection of skeletons, I came across a South American lizard called an iguana. Its teeth were shaped just like the one I had found, with the same ridges. The only difference was that my tooth was 20 times bigger.

This convinced me that I had indeed found a reptile. I decided to call my reptile *Iguanodon*, or "iguana tooth." ❖

Iguana
The South American iguana grows up to five feet (1.5 meters) long. Mantell pictured his *Iguanodon* like an iguana, but 20 times bigger.

Iguanodon
Mantell published his description of *Iguanodon* in 1825. It was the second dinosaur to be named.

19

Skeleton expert
Richard Owen was able to study many different skeletons by cutting up animals that died at London Zoo.

Crowd-pleaser
In 1854, huge crowds went to the Crystal Palace in London, to see the concrete models of *Iguanodon* and *Megalosaurus*.

Exhibition
Owen's models were the world's first dinosaur exhibition.

Dinner in a dinosaur

I will never forget the party I went to in London on New Year's Eve in 1853. We ate our dinner inside an *Iguanodon*!

It was not a flesh-and-blood *Iguanodon*, of course. It was a brick and concrete model, built to show the public what these remarkable beasts might have looked like.

My name is Prestwick and, like most of the guests on that evening, I'm a geologist.

At the head of the table sat our host, Professor Richard Owen, an expert on animal skeletons. He had designed the splendid creature in which we sat.

Owen rose to his feet and said, "Fellow scientists! Let us drink to the memory of Gideon Mantell, discoverer of *Iguanodon*!"

We raised our glasses and cried: "Mantell!" There was a brief silence, as we each remembered the good doctor, who had died the previous year. It was sad indeed that Mantell was not there, to see his discovery brought to life.

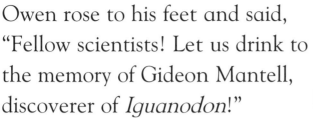

Thumb

Nose horn? The concrete *Iguanodon* had a horn on its nose. Mantell and Owen had both misunderstood this bone. It was really the dinosaur's thumb!

Straight legs
Straight legs
are better
at bearing
weight than
the sprawling
legs of lizards.
It was thanks
to their straight
legs that
dinosaurs could
grow so much
bigger than
any other
reptiles.

As midnight approached, my friend Professor Forbes thanked our host for the splendid meal.

Forbes said, "We owe Owen a great deal, gentlemen. Dr. Mantell and Professor Buckland thought of their discoveries as overgrown lizards. But in the 1830s, more bones of these huge reptiles were found, and Owen studied them closely.

"The Professor has a great understanding of skeletons.

He could see that, unlike lizards, these creatures held their bodies off the ground on straight legs. They were not giant lizards. They were a separate group of animals, which Owen has named *Dinosauria*.

And now, if I may," Forbes added, "I would like to read you a poem that I have written. It is about this magnificent *Iguanodon* in which we are sitting.

A thousand ages underground
His skeleton had lain;
But now his body's big and round
And he's himself again!
The jolly old beast
Is not deceased,
There's life in him again!"

At this, we all let out a huge roar like a bellowing herd of *Iguanodons*. ❖

Two legs or four?
Owen mistakenly believed that all dinosaurs walked on four legs. Later finds showed that many walked on their hind legs, like this *Giganotosaurus*.

Dinosaurs
In 1841, Owen invented the name "dinosaur." It means "terrible lizard" in Greek.

23

Expeditions
In the 1870s, Othniel Charles Marsh (1831–99) led his students on four fossil-hunting expeditions to the West.

Railroad
In the 1860s, the Union Pacific Railroad was built across the U.S.A., to link the cities of the East with the West.

The bone hunters

My name is Matthew Randall, but all my friends call me Matty. Let me tell you about my young days out in America's Wild West.

Back in 1868, I found work on the building of the Union Pacific Railroad. Laying those iron rails was hard work, and it was dangerous too.

This was the homeland of the Sioux Indians, who hated the railroad. Without the protection of the U.S. cavalry, we wouldn't have lasted very long.

For months on end, we lived on fried buffalo steaks, provided by our own hunter, "Buffalo Bill" Cody.

One day, a group of strangers rode into our camp. There were about a dozen youngsters led by an older fellow, who was short and plump.

"Good day," said the older man. "I am Professor Marsh of Yale University, and these are my students. We are on a bone-hunting expedition!"

This struck me as an odd occupation, although I was too polite to say so.

Buffalo Bill
William Cody earned his nickname by supplying the railway workers with buffalo meat. He was famous for his skill as a scout.

Sioux
The Sioux depended on buffalo for food, clothes, tools, and tents. The settlers and railroad ruined Sioux hunting grounds.

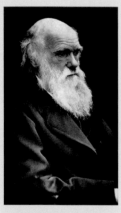
The professor had come to our camp to meet up with Buffalo Bill, who had offered to be his guide on the bone-hunting expedition.

Next morning, the bone-hunters rode off. Buffalo Bill led the way and Marsh rode beside him. They had an escort of cavalrymen and six wagons. We wished them well and then went back to our work on the railroad.

More than a month later, we met up with the professor again. His students now looked like real westerners, with tanned faces and well-worn clothing.

Marsh was full of stories of his adventures. He said that he'd shot an angry bull buffalo which was charging at him. He'd also made friends with some Sioux, who called him "Big Bone Chief."

Then he showed us the wagonloads of bones he'd collected.

He handed one of them around.

"Here's a real treasure," he said. "It's a bird's skull with teeth in its beak! This shows that birds must have evolved from reptiles. It proves that Darwin was right about evolution!"

We had no idea what he was talking about.

Bird with teeth
Darwin's followers believed that one group of dinosaurs grew feathers and took to the air. They evolved into birds. Early birds kept some reptile features, such as teeth.

Proof
Darwin's supporters hoped to find fossils that would prove his theory. This was why Marsh was excited to find a bird's skull with teeth.

Headdress
Sioux warriors wore eagle feather headdresses.

Black Hills
The Sioux fought for the Black Hills. They won a victory at the Battle of the Little Bighorn in 1877, but eventually they lost their territory.

The professor said that if we ever found any strange bones, we should write to him at Yale. Then he went home with his students and his collection of bones. I guessed that this was the last I would hear of bone-hunting.

Over the next years, big changes came to the West. The railroads I helped to build brought thousands of settlers from the East. New towns sprang up all over the place.

In 1874, gold was discovered in the Black Hills in Sioux territory. Soon, we had a real gold rush, with trainloads of easterners arriving, all hoping to strike it rich. The Sioux fought to defend their land, but were forced to move to reservations.

I'd found a job looking after the train depot at a little place called Como Bluff in Wyoming. I had plenty of free time and I'd often walk up into the hills. There wasn't much to look at there – just a lot of dry, bare rocks.

But one day in 1877, I found a bone sticking out of the rocks that

was bigger than I was! Nearby, there was another huge bone, and another. These bones seemed to go on for miles.

Teepees
Before they were forced to stay on reservations, the Sioux made good use of portable homes called teepees. These were made of buffalo hide stretched over wooden poles.

Bare rocks
The rocky hills of Wyoming have been worn away by rivers, rain, and wind. These areas, called badlands, are wonderful places to find fossils.

Cope
Edward Drinker Cope (1840–97) wrote over 1,400 books and articles and named more than a 1,000 new animal species.

Spies
Both Marsh and Cope hired spies to keep an eye on what the other one was doing. They also used bribes to win over diggers from the rival team.

I was going to send a letter to Marsh, but then I heard that a rich bone-hunting professor had arrived in Canon City, not far away.

I traveled there, expecting to find Marsh. But I was surprised to see a different fellow. He said his name was Edward Drinker Cope.

I asked him if he knew Marsh. "Marsh!" shouted Cope, turning red in the face. "The man is a fraud and a thief!" It seemed that Cope hated Marsh worse than poison.

When I told him about the bones I had found, he offered me $100.

I had to show him the place, and keep it a secret from Marsh's spies.

Cope soon had a team of diggers at work, blasting the rock with gunpowder and prying the bones out with crowbars. Many bones shattered and were thrown away.

But Cope couldn't keep his secret for ever. One day a team of Marsh's diggers showed up. It was just like the days of the gold rush, only these fellows were after bones. ❖

Broken bones
Eventually the diggers invented ways to protect the bones they dug up. Marsh's men wrapped them in strips of cloth, soaked in flour and water. Cope's men used boiled rice instead of flour.

Useful technique
The practice of wrapping fossils in cloth and plaster of Paris is still used on some digs today.

Feud
Marsh and Cope fell out when Marsh pointed out that Cope had reconstructed a sea reptile with its head on the end of its tail. This humiliated Cope, who never forgave Marsh.

Heavy reptile
Barosaurus belonged to the sauropod family of dinosaurs, which were the largest animals ever to walk the Earth.

The great bone rush

Cope and Marsh each had teams of diggers working all over the West. It was a race to describe and name the new species. As a result of this "bone rush," they discovered almost 130 new kinds of dinosaur.

Cope worked alone, but Marsh had a team of expert assistants to help him put the skeletons together.

Marsh's dinosaurs came in many shapes and sizes. There was the flesh-eating *Allosaurus* ("different reptile") and gigantic plant-eaters like the *Barosaurus* ("heavy reptile").

Triceratops

There were also dinosaurs with horns, such as the *Triceratops* ("three-horned face").

The strangest dinosaur of all was one Marsh called *Stegosaurus* ("roofed reptile"). It had rows of mysterious bony plates all along its back.

Meanwhile, Cope and Marsh attacked each other in newspaper articles. Their squabbling made both of them look silly, but it also made "dinosaur" a household word. ❖

Roofed reptile
Scientists still argue about what the *Stegosaurus* used its plates for. Some think they helped the animal control its temperature. Others believe they were used to signal to other dinosaurs.

Allosaurus

Stegosaurus

Life's work
Werner Janensch (1878–1969) spent the rest of his life working on the bones he brought back from Africa.

Leg bone
Brachiosaurus was so big that its femur (upper leg bone) was as long as a person!

The biggest bone dig

My name is Dr. Werner Janensch. I've just come home to Germany after spending three years in Africa, leading a huge dig.

Back in 1907, I heard that some giant bones had been found at a place called Tendugaru in East Africa. I raised the money for an expedition and sailed to Africa in 1909.

I hired hundreds of local workers to do the digging. Tendugaru lies far inland, and there are no roads. All our food and supplies had to be carried on foot from the coast. The bones we dug up had to be carried back in the same way.

I was expecting to find new dinosaurs in Africa.

We've come back with more than 80,000 dinosaur bones. Now I've got to try to sort them out!

The baffling thing is that my bones belong to the *Brachiosaurus* and other species that have also been found in America. Africa and America are separated by the wide Atlantic Ocean. How did these lumbering beasts get from one continent to the other?

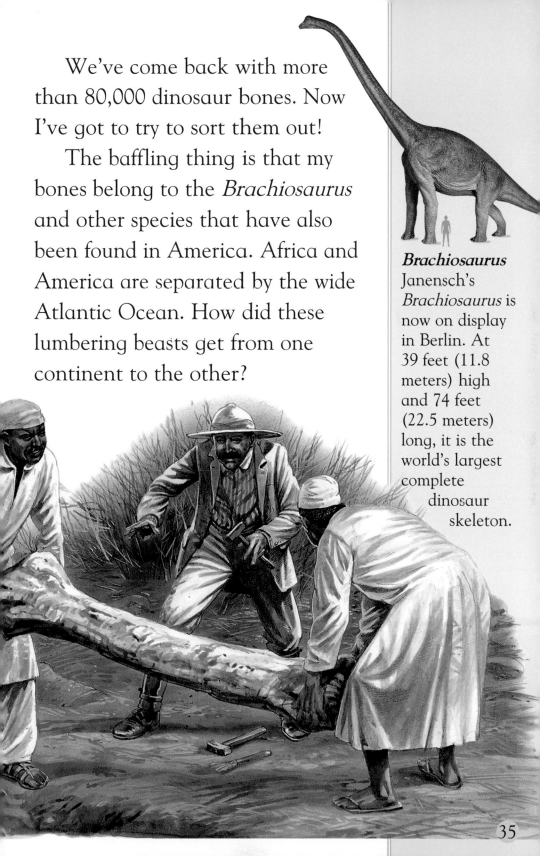

Brachiosaurus
Janensch's *Brachiosaurus* is now on display in Berlin. At 39 feet (11.8 meters) high and 74 feet (22.5 meters) long, it is the world's largest complete dinosaur skeleton.

Wegener
In 1912, Alfred Wegener suggested that there was once only one huge land mass which he called "Pangaea." He believed that it had split into pieces. The pieces slowly drifted apart to form the continents that we know today.

Wild theory
At the time, few scientists took Wegener's theory of "continental drift" seriously. It was not until the 1960s that he was proved right.

In Berlin, I showed my *Brachiosaurus* skull to some of our geologists. "This is an American dinosaur," I explained. "How did it end up in Africa? It's a mystery!"

Most of them were puzzled. But a young man called Alfred Wegener said, "It's not a mystery at all. This is exactly the type of dinosaur I would expect to find in Africa!"

Wegener pulled out a world map. "Look at the coastlines of Africa and South America.

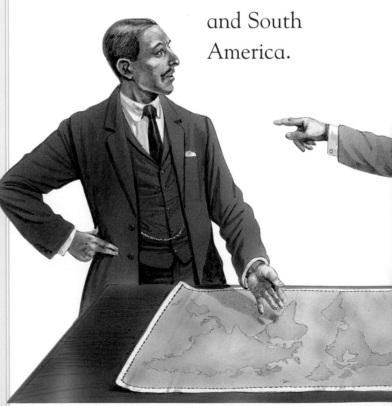

Their shapes match exactly. I believe that they must have once been joined. Somehow, they have drifted to their present positions.

This is why you found the same dinosaurs in Africa and America. When your *Brachiosaurus* was alive, there was no Atlantic Ocean!"

We were all startled by this wild theory. "Are you seriously suggesting that continents can roam around the Earth's surface?" I asked.

"How is this possible?" "I don't know," said Wegener. "But your *Brachiosaurus* is the proof that I am right!" ❖

Drifting continents
We now know that the Earth's surface is made up of several enormous plates floating on top of molten rock. Forces inside the Earth move the plates slowly. This is what made the continents move and split apart.

270 million years ago

130 million years ago

Present day

37

Triassic
(248–205 million years ago)
Early dinosaurs, like this small *Herrerasaurus,* evolved in the Triassic period.

Jurassic
(205–144 million years ago)
Dinosaurs like *Diplodocus* reached their largest size and dominated the whole Earth.

Dating the dinosaurs

Like detectives, early geologists collected evidence to piece together the story of life on Earth. Using fossils, they were able to place different periods of the Earth's history in order. They gave these periods names based on the type of rocks in which the various fossils were found.

The age of the dinosaurs was divided into three periods: Triassic, when dinosaurs first evolved; Jurassic, when they became the main land animals; and Cretaceous, when new sorts, such as the horned dinosaurs, appeared.

Geologists knew that Triassic dinosaurs must have lived before Jurassic ones.

But they could only guess how long ago that was.

It was not until the 1920s that scientists were able to work out the age of rocks. This was thanks to the study of radioactivity.

Many rocks are made up of elements which are radioactive. These elements slowly decay, or break down, to form other elements. Scientists measure the amount of a radioactive element in a rock. They can then work out how long the decay has been going on and so when the rock was formed.

Radioactive decay is like a clock, ticking away inside the Earth's rocks. Using this clock, scientists were able to date the rocks holding the dinosaur fossils.

This told them when the dinosaurs had lived. ❖

Cretaceous
(144–65 million years ago)
This was the age of the horned dinosaurs, such as this *Protoceratops.*

Elements
Elements are the basic substances, such as carbon and iron, that all things are made of. Radioactive elements include potassium and uranium.

Jack Horner
Dr. Jack
Horner (1946–)
is one of the
world's leading
experts on
dinosaurs.
He was the
technical
adviser for the
films *Jurassic
Park* and *The
Lost World.*

Paleontology
A modern
dinosaur
detective is
called a
paleontologist.
Paleontology
is the study
of ancient life.
It comes from
the Greek
word, *palaios*,
which means
"ancient."

Baby dinosaurs

In 1978, a paleontologist named Jack Horner was visiting a fossil shop in Montana, U.S.A. He found the bones of a baby dinosaur. This was an important discovery. Few baby dinosaurs had ever been found!

Horner traced the fossil back to the rocky hillside where it had been discovered, and began to dig. Soon he had uncovered a huge nest. It was over 6 feet (2 meters) wide and contained 15 baby dinosaurs and lots of crushed eggshells.

In the 1980s, Horner's team found more nests at the site. Some of them contained eggs and newly hatched babies.

Horner knew that the soil around the nests could hold clues.

By sifting the soil and examining it under a microscope, he discovered the remains of chewed up leaves and berries. He also found dinosaur droppings, containing woody debris from conifer trees. Can you work out what he discovered?

Horner used these clues and other evidence to build an amazing picture of the lives of these dinosaurs.

Fossilized baby Horner's team chipped away the rock to discover this fossilized eggshell containing a baby hatchling.

Jack Horner's most important discovery was that the babies were being looked after by their parents. He called this dinosaur *Maiasaura*, which means "good mother lizard."

The evidence for parental care was the size of the 15 babies. Since they were three times bigger than newly hatched ones, they must have stayed in their nest for weeks after hatching.

Herds
Fossil footprints are further evidence that some dinosaurs, such as these *Gallimimus*, traveled in herds. The young stayed in the middle of a herd, while the adults walked on either side, for protection.

They had crushed the eggshells in their nest as they moved around. The chewed up leaves and berries were food brought by the parents.

The mystery is why the babies died. Perhaps something happened to their parents and the babies starved to death in the nest.

In 1984, Horner's team made another discovery. They found the bones of 10,000 *Maiasaura* that had been killed by a volcanic eruption. Finding so many animals together shows that they lived in huge herds. ❖

Like modern animals
Jack Horner says, "Dinosaurs basically aren't any different from animals alive today. They just looked different."

Nest site
Horner thinks that these *Maiasaura* returned to the same nest site year after year, just like many birds and turtles do today.

End of the dinosaurs

Sixty-five million years ago, the dinosaurs disappeared. No one knows for certain why this happened, nor why some other animals, such as mammals and fish, survived.

Scientists do know that the Earth's climate was cooling down at the time. If dinosaurs were cold-blooded, like modern reptiles, they may have been unable to cope with the cold weather.

Warm-blooded mammals could have taken over.

In 1990, a huge crater about 124 miles (200 kilometers) across was found on the seabed off Mexico. It was formed 65 million years ago when a massive object, such as an meteorite, crashed into the Earth.

The impact of such a large meteorite would throw up a huge cloud of dust and gases. This would block out the Sun's light for months. Without sunlight, plants would die, followed by the animals that ate them. Perhaps this is what led to the end of the dinosaurs. ❖

Warm-blooded
People, lemurs, and other warm-blooded animals control their body temperature by converting food into heat. They need more food than cold-blooded animals.

Meteorites
Meteorites are rocks which hurtle through space, occasionally smashing into the Earth.

Tyrannosaurus rex
T.rex ("king tyrant lizard") was a huge meat-eating dinosaur, up to 20 feet (6 meters) high and 40 feet (12 meters) long. It lived in the late Cretaceous period.

Smell
T.rex used its sense of smell to track down food – either living animals to hunt, or animals that had already died.

Today's detectives

When Mary Anning went fossil hunting, her only equipment was a geological hammer. But today's dinosaur detectives have many more tools at their disposal.

In 1998, scientists in California used computers and X-rays to study the skull of a *Tyrannosaurus rex*. They scanned it for 500 hours. They produced hundreds of computerized images. These pictures revealed that the dinosaur had huge olfactory lobes – the parts of the brain used for smell. *T.rex* clearly had a powerful nose!

Dinosaur modeling has come a long way since the concrete *Iguanodon* in 1853. Today, experts examine fossils for marks where muscles were attached.

These show the modelers how to shape the body and how the animal moved. Even so, much is guesswork: fossils can't show us the color of skin or eyes.

People are still hunting for dinosaurs and new species are being discovered. Perhaps, lying in the rocks beneath your feet, there are the bones of unknown dinosaurs. ❖

Computers
Thanks to computer animation, we can see how dinosaurs moved in films such as *Jurassic Park* and in museum displays around the world.

Glossary

Ammonite
A prehistoric sea creature with a coiled shell. Ammonites are among the most common fossils.

Cold-blooded
To have a body temperature that varies with the surroundings. Reptiles and fish are cold-blooded.

Continental drift
The theory that the continents were once joined together, but split apart and slowly drifted to their present positions.

Cretaceous
The third period in the age of the dinosaurs, 144–65 million years ago.

Dinosaurs
Land reptiles that lived between 248–65 million years ago. Many dinosaurs were very big. The name dinosaur means "terrible lizard" in Greek.

Elements
The basic substances, such as hydrogen, carbon, and iron, that all things are made of.

Evolution
The theory that species of animals and plants gradually change over long periods of time to produce new species.

Extinction
The complete dying out of a species.

Fossils
Traces of animals and plants, preserved in rocks. Fossils include bones, skin, and footprints. The name means "dug up" in Latin.

Geology
The study of the Earth and its rocks.

Jurassic
The second period in the age of the dinosaurs, 205–144 million years ago.

Mammals
A group of warm-blooded animals with hair. Mammals give birth to live young, which they feed on milk. Mice, whales, horses, and humans are mammals.

Meteorites
Large rocks that hurtle through space and occasionally smash into the Earth.

Naturalist
A scientist who studies animals and plants.

Paleontology
The study of ancient life, from the Greek word, *palaios*, which means "ancient."

Pterosaurs
Flying reptiles that lived at the same time as the dinosaurs.

Quarry
A place where stone is dug out of the ground.

Radioactivity
The energy released by elements, such as uranium, as they slowly break down, or decay. Radioactivity can be used to date rocks.

Reptiles
A group of cold-blooded, egg-laying animals with scaly skins. They include lizards, snakes, tortoises, and crocodiles.

Sauropods
A group of huge, long-necked dinosaurs that included *Barosaurus*.

Species
A group of animals or plants that can breed together and that differ only in minor details.

Triassic
The first period in the age of the dinosaurs, 248–205 million years ago.

Warm-blooded
To have a body that stays constantly warm. Mammals are warm-blooded.